Entrepreneur Bible to Riches

The Gospel of Wealth Attraction

by Dan Moskel

ISBN-13:
978-1496188816

ISBN-10:
1496188810

Other Books By Dan Moskel

Video Marketing For Entrepreneurs

Email Marketing That Works ... So You Don't Have To

The Blueprint to Affiliate Marketing

How To Create a Website Easy Button

SEO Training Manual - The 10 Golden Steps To Shower In Search Engine Traffic

* Grab a free treasure trove of wealth building tools at DanMoskelUniversity.com

Table of Contents

Chapter 1.

The Red Pill or The Blue Pill

Listen, the Entrepreneur's Bible is not some formal religious text, giving you a quick hit of some feel-good new age thinking or metaphysical B.S.

This book contains, the gospel and plain truth to living the good life, to success as an entrepreneur, and attracting wealth faster, than baseball players on steroids break Babe Ruth's home run record.

You see I grew up in the church, the son of a preacher man. I can recall sitting in Sunday school and the church bells just didn't sing, true for me, hearing about Adam and Eve in the garden of eden, talking to snakes.

For that sounds a bit like: e-meters, coming back in the next life as a cat, and bloomers, or special panties will protect the mormons from fire, knives, and when bullets fly about.

You see, most of what you've been told about success and wealth, is wrong. The idea that if you're just a "better" or more moral person, then you would be more deserving of success, is pure unadulterated blasphemy.

Sure, it sounds nice. But, it doesn't matter how moral, good, or positive your thinking gets, if that's your plan, your wishing upon on a shooting star, and may as well invest with your credit card in lottery tickets.

While the metaphysical fruit-loops may be OK performing this hippie witchcraft, and retreating into the forest, to eat their granola bars, I'm not.

You see, the politicians seem to be interested in distracting the herd with our so called war on drugs, fighting inequality, and complaining about Mark Cuban, and Mr. Burns paying their "fair share."

In our brave new economy the rules have changed. To encourage you to take my words seriously, let me briefly share my qualifications.

While the talking heads on TV have been busy banging pots and pans about the latest financial crisis, our great recession, health care, and George Bush's last apocalyptic, passage of gas.

Starting from zero financial resources, no lucky breaks, or silver spoons. As a college dropout, I've climbed up to earn millions of dollars, all working from comfort of home, since 2006.

I've been jet setting, all over the world, from riding horseback in the jungles of Belize, to feeding elephants in the bustling streets of Bangkok, out to the Wynn in Las Vegas for a Tiesto show, then up to NYC for March Madness at Madison Square Garden.

You may have even seen me on national TV. I appeared in my own infomercial, on ESPN, MTV, VH-1, Comedy Central, to name just a few.

You see, the herd seems to believe honest, moral, hard work, and long hours, or black vodoo magic, are the only paths to wealth.

But this is not the gospel. The plain truth is this belief is blasphemous to wealth attraction.

This is the forsaken path it will leave you broke, destitute, and hoping to get lucky with your credit card investment in this weeks mega million dollar sweepstakes drawing.

Look, in this book, I'm going to reveal all the dirty little secrets to shift your perspective from merely making money, to attracting wealth, success, and living the good life, in less time than you ever thought possible, and without selling your soul to the devil.

You see attracting wealth is similar to men searching to pick up women. It much more fruitful, if you work on making yourself attractive to women.

I've yet to here of a shortage of women, now that would be apocalyptic breaking news!

Can I get an amen, because the southern baptist church bells are ringing, with the gospel, on that plain truth.

Listen, money is governed by cause and effect, not honest, back breaking hard work, or any individuals moral codes.

This is why criminals, drug dealers, and gun runners, can amass extravagant amounts of wealth.

Warning

Yes, a warning, this is a shocking, and blunt revelation of the gospel of wealth attraction, and the plain truth to the abundance of riches.

It will offend the meek, and if you cling to the delusional belief in a fantasyland, of unicorns, and leprechauns, where money, let alone mankind follow moral laws. And getting rich quick, is a deadly sin, it's not too late, to turn back now.

But, if your ready to get on board the golden path to the good life, filled with abundant riches, overflowing with success and achievement, then climb aboard, for fortunes, don't wait for the tardy to arrive.

Or you can continue to plod along, as just one more among the herd, on the well traveled dead end path to poverty, frustration, and bitterness with Mr. Burns.

In the movie The Matrix, Keanu Reeves was given a choice to take the red pill or the blue pill. Right now, this moment, your faced with the same decision, what choice will you make?

Buckle up, if your one of the few, brave, courageous souls, ready to take your place in the money race. And come along to rise to the top, because your life won't ever be the same.

Make haste, go now and gather ye fellow Flanderinos together, for our first tale begins with ... The Origin of Life.

Chapter 2.

The Origin of Life

Did your heart just start beating a little bit faster, don't worry, the gospel is not here to sway your view, one way or another.

But, have you noticed, people seem to go into wild hysteria, and flail about like a rabid squirrel dropped in a bucket of maple syrup, anytime this topic comes about?

On a recent trip, with my Dad to Charleston, South Carolina, a neat, historic, port city, in America. We attended a lecture by a leading thinker in the intelligent design movement, Michael Behe, author of Darwin's Black Box.

You see, a lot of people get so worked up, so heated over this debate, so wrapped up in being right, and what's right for our kids to learn, they file lawsuits, call each other names, and go to all lengths to "prove" the other is wrong.

Here's the thing, at the end of the day, regardless, if we evolved from the great apes or not, the gospel says we all still have to eat today.

For the plain truth is mankind does cope well with the pain of hunger, and is much happier with a full stomach.

So while others spend major time, worrying about the right answer, to a question that is at best, interesting to thee.

Shouldn't you and I be busy earning a living or in what past civilizations was seen as the most useful skill, and be out hunting?

If only to feed ourself, and should someone ever find the proof, I'm not all that interested in hearing about it.

At least not until after I've done my hunting for the day, for the gospel and the plain truth in life says, I'll be hungry later. Regardless, of any high alert discovery, you've found of we.

Mankind, is so engulfed in this debate, the fumes cloud our vision, from seeing what lies right, in front of us.

This is sure to offend, the herd, but this tenet is liberating and the application to mankind in business, and it's behavior is priceless.

For now you can cast off the heavy chains of false beliefs, built by the imprisoned herd.

Take heed, for the gospel says to momentarily shed your fragile human ego.

You must listen, carefully and objectively to put these pieces together, to fully absorb this plain truth.

You see, intelligent design and evolution, are both right. Research has found Neanderthal humans, and hobbit like people, but this isn't why evolution is right.

After all the idea that a big bang just happened, seems about as likely as man living in a fish, elephants mating with humans, and Joseph Smith being abducted by aliens.

The Lord of the Ants

Have you heard of E.O. Wilson? He's is a scientist, that specialized in studying ants! He discovered ant's have societies and civilizations.

There is a queen ant, and worker ant, just like in the Pixar film a Bug's Life. Surely, you've heard about the queen bee, and worker bees?

You see, E. O. Wilson discovered that ants communicate with one another, just like our kind.

They communicate very sophisticated messages, even a societies class structure to the others of their kind.

Did you know when one ant finds a food supply, he will communicate to the other ants, using chemicals, in his butt, and leave a trail for the other ants to follow to the food.

In fact, many members of the animal kingdom, have been found, to communicate with the others in their herd.

Did you read the Kurt Vonnegut book, Welcome To The Monkey House?

It is a collection of short stories, and one particularly entertaining, and thought provoking story, tells how dogs communicate telepathically with humans.

And how these furry, four legged felines, are really the masters of mankind.

Surprisingly, this seems pretty reasonable when you look at all our kind does for our furry four legged friends and family members: we feed them, walk them, bathe them, love them, protect them.

And heck, even leave them inheritances, like the wealthy widow a few years back, in New York City.

You see, every dog owner, at one time or another has experienced the phenomena, of their dog telling them something, if only it's time to go outside to water the lawn.

You see, if dogs are the masters of mankind, it's OK, they worth hunting a little extra for.

Look at all they provide our kind, alerting a family the house is on fire, protecting us from would be intruders, trying to fight off bears for residents in Alaska, and helping the blind navigate in the world, not to mention all the intangibles of companionship.

The point is, while the herd is busy arguing about evolution or intelligent design. It sure seems reasonable, that we can assume the evidence points to the plain truth that man has evolved from primates.

Despite, the pain this causes our fragile ego.

But, this in no way disproves the existence of God, or natural selection. The evidence and E.O. Wilson seem to only bolster the existence of a God, or lord almighty Big Banger.

You see, if all animals have the ability to form societies, communicate with one another, work cooperatively, and even individual members of each species have a class structure, serving specific functions and providing unique contributions to the herd.

Then, doesn't it only pose the bigger question ... of what's the purpose of life?

After all, we know plants are alive.

Chapter 3.

Moral Monkey Money

Just as if you were to try and explain to your dog to be just and moral, money is a creation of man.

Thus, the gospel says, money doesn't follow mankind's morals or ethical codes.

For animals show kindness, caring for one another, protecting one another, but they also steal from one anther, and fight bitterly with each other, just like our kind.

In the belief, we can make the world reflect an idea of our own creating, is like hoping our dog will be fair and just when chasing the neighbors cat.

We cannot get mankind to follow, any set of moral laws or ethics. And the plain truth is the rest of the world, don't have the same comprehension or understanding of fairness, as we.

Just as every member of man defines fair in a different way, than thee. For the rules change quick when you start taking away man's food. Let alone, take away his afternoon talk show with Gerry Springala.

It's not hard to make a case that our kind has been pretty unfair, to all other life on earth.

This IS ... just what is. We don't have to explain it all, have reasons for everything. Can we not all just be?

Don't be such a nervous monkey, to commit the only sin. For the gospel says to relax, laugh heartily, play like a child ape, and enjoy your time along your journey in life.

Instead, of frantically searching for answers to questions that our kind, may not even be able to comprehend, or recognize, if were to find thee.

It sure seems reasonable to suppose we don't need to know, or maybe we're looking to hard to see.

For is it not a plain truth, that every child can see and has wondered, if the animals have their own little worlds, just like we.

The gospel says to break free the bonds of false belief that money responds to morals, ethics, wishes, or goes to need.

Money simply moves from one person to another, one entity to another.

There is no first checking with moral right or wrongs before the movement, it does not stop at a stoplight, like we.

And it does not move according to mankind's interpretation of fair and just.

This is why the monkey spending his time scheming on a way to get Ms. Jackson's food, will never be a valued member of the kind.

He is too concerned with getting something for free, and has chosen to go along a forsaken well traveled path, ending in bitterness with Mr. Burns.

For he can't see all he has to do, is go out and hunt for his own food. I'll even show him how.

The plaint truth is organized crime, governments, and individual people, who go through life taking things by force, instead of through cooperative effort, always find tough opposition.

For the gospel says there is plenty for us all, and that is what the lord high almighty Big Banger, intended for his creations, mankind, the animal kingdom, and all of life!

For don't waste this precious gift, trying to steal or force Ms. Jackson to give her food to thee.

Instead, just come along with me, and we can go hunt together and both eat a feast tonight, and have plenty left over, to invite her to share in our feast for three.

After all, she is such a delight to be, and has some of the most interesting stories, and you know it was her brother, who taught our uncle how to hunt ... and he taught me how to hunt, and today I taught you how to hunt, make sure tomorrow you teach another monkey, how to hunt, so we can all continue to rejoice and eat!

Just as science, is searching for the little differences that make the big difference between mankind, and the great apes.

It is the little daily disciplines, that make all the difference, over the course of a lifetime, in building the good life.

Or wasting you time, spinning your wheels, wishing money would go to need, and trying to change the laws of the lord almighty Big Banger.

Let us not allow the lazy monkeys in our troop to distract us, from achieving our purpose in life.

Even if they are screaming, jumping up and down, stomping and pounding their chest about how we aren't giving a "fair share" of our hunt to thee.

It's OK if, they can't hunt because of Gerry Springala and a six pack of duff beer, is just too darn entertaining. For I heard they're even racing them fancy, fast cars, round in that big circle after Gerry.

Sure Homer ... you may also like this bone from the feast, we had last night, you may want to use it to bang on your drum, while me and the others take delight in the hunt for thee.

I'm telling you, hunting is way more fun. You should really just try it, someday ... you might just like it!

Chapter 4.

Look Objectively

You see, mankind has a BIG ego. This get's in the way of seeing, and learning the lessons our lord Big Banger, left in plain sight for us all to see.

If you can separate yourself from the emotions, and the ego that come along with being man.

And not look to judge everything, and everyone, by your own moral guide, and ethical code.

You'll see it doesn't take a rocket scientist, to see how mankind, behave very similarly to the animals, the gorillas, dogs, sheep, and every living thing.

I'm not singing kum-bay-yaa, and prancing off into the forest here.

Merely, trying to point out, being able to see objective here, the way animals behave, and apply that to mankind, makes life, business, and finding an explanation for the other monkeys behavior, much easier to find.

It's frustrating to go through life, trying to project and hope everyone and everything in the world, would only just live by your personal definition of moral, ethics, right and wrong.

If things worked this way, we would have no prisons, no criminals, no violence, and no laws. We would all be living in a utopian, garden of eden among the leprechauns, and riding unicorns, along rainbows.

For the gospel says belief in a creator, cosmic force, or divine intervention can benefit you on your journey in life, success, and wealth.

After all, we had to start with some form of Big Banger, go now and gather ye fellow Flanderinos together, and cast off the heavy bonds the handicapping beliefs the herd, drapes upon our kind.

The plain truth is man and wealth are not good or bad, it just is. Now, let's get busy learning from it, so we can rise to the top, and stop following the mainstream, popular herds beliefs of scarcity, lack, and need.

We know they want to busy themselves trying to rule mankind and money, by laws of their own making. Instead of simply following, the universal laws of the almighty Big Banger.

And just in case you think, I'm some liberal, bleeding heart, wanting to sit about in a circle, holding hands with the panda bears and fart.

Did you know even the monkeys, cast out the criminals in their society, very similar to how humans put criminals in prison, in today's society.

I'm simply one of the productive hunters among our troop, come along and join our tribe, for you can sleep as soundly as the little baby apes at night, in the plain truth, for it it wasn't for us ... NO ONE, WOULD EAT!

Chapter 5.

Shades of Grey

Is it not wildly entertaining when the eggheads, claim humans are so superior and different from the animal kingdom, because animals don't have language, can't communicate, etc.

But, isn't mankind trying to study the way in which monkeys communicate, kind of like, dogs trying to study the way in which, ants communicate.

And because ants don't bark reaching the conclusion, that ants don't have language.

For the gospel says for us to enjoy the challenge of the hunt, and the overflowing confidence, power, and self-reliance, that comes along with being the most valuable member of your kind, a producer.

Certainly, being the fittest, at least, helps our chances for survival. History shows under difficult conditions, the most vulnerable members of every species, are the first to pay the price.

Starting with children, then elderly, then women, and last ending with the most useful, the producing hunters.

For the gospel reminds us to not be so arrogant to forget, we were once children and vulnerable ourself.

And the lucky of us, may be vulnerable again as we go through our journey in life. Trading in youth for age and wisdom, which is a far superior choice, than the alternative trade for youth.

Let us, also be wise enough, to teach other gorillas how to hunt today, for we know not what tomorrow will bring.

We may need them to feed us, should we find ourself vulnerable again, even as a wise, old gorilla.

We can all learn one important plain truth from the animals, they do take care of one another.

And while some among mankind may want to speculate if they do this in a fair, or unfair way.

That's like saying the world is all black and white, when it's really only shades of gray!

For, Isaac Newton discovered that the shade or color white, is not an absence of colors, but rather all the colors of the rainbow.

The Lion King tells us about a circle of life, and certainly you've heard the saying about how each of us need all of us, and all of us need each of us.

Why then would we exclude our furry four legged friends, or the plants, and not bring along the whole animal kingdom.

For the gospel says don't you and the herd like to eat steak, fried chicken, corn, and mashed potatoes. Heck, I even like to have some cherry pie, and a glass of milk for dessert.

The plain truth is the plants and animals are the raw materials of life. It is the source of the food you eat, the products man creates, and essential to the services, mankind sell to one another.

For we must hunt the cougar and the deer, but they must first eat the grasses, and other animals before they are big and fat enough, to feed us.

The idea of fairness, is just like language, government, and religion, it has been built by man. And since man is fallible, then so to, could be all his creations.

If your a connoisseur of history, your certainly aware of all the right bounces Christianity, got along the path to become such a powerful force in mankind.

If not, go check it out, especially if you claim to be a Christian. But this also applies to every religion, go look through history and see what it is responsible for.

If the stories sound like experiences today, or it sounds more like your listening to the movie Cars. Then you have to reach your own conclusions, and proceed with what works best for maximum productivity with your life.

If you study Sociology, it is fascinating to see how knowledge is passed from one generation to the next.

Did you know every society in recorded history, creates their idea and belief in a higher power?

All the way back to the Incan sun gods, to greek mythology, even to Joseph Smith being abducted by aliens.

If you look at knowledge before the written word, let alone the English language, you can see that it was passed through sitting round ye fire telling tales, just like today's families gather round ye TV's.

But, in the past they would share religious tales.

For the gospel says, come on man, it's pretty hard to beat, raising your arms and parting a sea, defeating Goliath with a slingshot, or battling the raging waters in an ark.

These colorful additives, is what keeps the lessons, of our kind alive, and passing from one generation to the next, along the road of civilization, as ye know it.

Further, a plain truth of mankind is if not for these colorful additives, it would only be something else the gorilla troop would be bickering about today.

At the 2004 presidential primary convention, where I was the handler for senator Bob Graham of Florida, I overheard a high ranking leading monkey of the Democratic party, roll back on his heels, and say to thee:

"*My boy, everything is entertainment, even politics.*"

Chapter 6.

Money, Money, Money, Everywhere ...

It's shocking to see the discomfort, money produces in people. Just talking about it, spending it, investing it, even quoting prices produces massive discomfort for the herd.

Heck, even being given money, look at all the lawsuits, family squabbles, and ended relationships over a family inheritance!

For the gospel says there is plenty of money everywhere. It's all around us. In America, we print more money, every single day!

Currently, in the United States there is a massive shift of wealth. The baby boomers are aging and according to some experts, over 60% of the wealth in America, is contained in this generation.

In the coming years, there will be a huge surge in products and services created for, and marketed specifically to this demographic.

This opportunity and growing market will be capitalized on by many smart entrepreneurs.

Take heed, and avoid running with the herd and their false belief our economy is bad, job opportunity has been outsourced to China, money is scarce, the world should be fair, or fighting inequality is a worthy cause.

The is blasphemous of the wealth attraction gospel.

For the plain truth is the politicians pander to these ideas to win votes, and if you look at history, the media is continuously clamoring we are in a never before seen, war of the worlds type catastrophe, as often as George Bush in a monkey speech, would forget about being fooled.

At no other time in history, have we had so much technology available to us, to help us break free of the work money link.

The plain truth is, thanks to this technology, working even part time, from home today, anyone can build passive recurring revenue streams that crank out monkey money, as reliably as any great apes, grandfather clock.

For the gospel, shows us there is no shortage of opportunity, simply a shortage of monkeys in the troop, willing to do what it takes!

Revelations, show that these men, prefer to spend exponentially more energy, building invisible pillars of arrogance, dishonesty, and hypocrisy, supporting the foundation of the poverty stricken, victim of the world mentality.

Which quickly leaves them feeling as hopeless as a prisoner, left stranded on a pacific island, after the apocalyptic war of the worlds, and decimation of all your fellow monkey-kind.

The plain truth is today, it doesn't even require capital to get started, a few easy and inexpensive ways to begin, is to start now sharing your knowledge with others.

You can write books, build a website, create YouTube videos, sell other peoples products and services, and a million and half other ways to earn money with your existing knowledge and skills, RIGHT NOW!

Being lucky enough to be an American, means you've been given the best chance, simply by being born in the right place.

This gives you the opportunity, and opportunity is all anyone can ask for, hope for, or have.

Everyday you can take advantage of it, and take action to create, build, and make the good life, have your dream career, family relationships, travel, you name it, you can make it happen, if you start right bloody monkey now.

Napolean Hill once said:

"*The man of decision gets what he goes after, no matter how long it takes, no matter how difficult the task. The man of decision cannot be stopped. The man of indecision cannot be started.*"

I first started in business, at 21 only months before the "credit crisis" in America, in the financial industry albeit. I was earning consistently $5,000.00 a week, living like a rockstar!

And overnight my business was crippled, along with my income. But, I was able to peek my head out, above the herd and see what is possible!

I learned more skills, and made myself more valuable to the market. This was a problem berthing opportunity, one of many, in the journey of business, riches, and success.

Despite the monkey government watching a 20/20 episode and passing, new legislation in this industry, that ultimately created a more predatory lending market for the others, and was immediately worked around by the high priced financial monkey attorneys.

Once again, I brushed aside, momentary defeat to climb back to the top of the herd, figuring it out, and creating a very lucrative, recurring income stream in this industry.

All while selling other monkeys products and services, for them! Yup, you heard that correctly, no customer service, no client headaches, no credit card processing, and no more time in monkey meetings!

All I need is an internet connection, and a computer to go on the hunt and feed the troop ... and this is all you need to!

For the gospel shows countless others before us did this using pen and paper. Same idea, just a different form of media.

If writing isn't for you, you can do video, today. But, you gotta get busy, with the tools you have on hand, to catch any of that monkey money.

These tools have provided me the opportunity to earn an affluent income, from home, and even part time, while I returned and finished college with marks on the deans list, all while earning more money than my monkey professors!

You see, money is nothing more than numbers on a screen and funny looking paper ... NOTHING MORE!

The gospel says there is nothing to fear with money, being around it, and having huge sums of it, in your midst.

Look, I like to have money all around me, tucking balls of cash in nooks and crannies all over my habitat.

The plain truth is this helps to program your subconscious to always be thinking of how you can be of more service to the other monkeys.

For the gospel teaches us, as reliably as the sun rises in the east and sets in the west, when your of more service to the others, you shall dance and rejoice as a monkey and let the riches rain down upon you.

For this is a universal law of the almighty Big Banger, it will endure beyond the birds and the bees.

It's as reliable to govern the movement of money as Newtons law of gravity, and Einsteins theory of relativity.

For as long as their is summer, spring, fall, and winter, this law will be indelibly etched in granite in all of mankind, and is the natural order of life.

The plain truth is sometimes, monkeys get so locked in routine, habit, and the hopelessness of the imprisonment of poverty, they only reinforce these gates, by believing they can change this plain truth.

Have you ever seen a religious leader, government official, or athlete render gravity ineffective?

Me neither, we would haul them off and lock them away, with all the other crazy monkeys, for even trying.

Gene Simmons of the rock band KISS says:

"Be clear, be truthful. Stand there proudly, unapologetically, unabashedly, and say, 'I love cash. It will get me everything I want in life.' "

Despite the clear and dramatic differences in the depression and what the media has deemed our "Great Recession."

The plain truth is, everyday fortunes are amassing, new businesses being launched, and we live in time with a level of disposable income in the world, beyond any earlier monkeys wildest dreams.

Chapter 7.

Our Brave New Economy

In our brave new economy, despite what the politicians may say, or even like to believe, the world is NOT fair today, yesterday, or tomorrow.

It doesn't matter what type of government is in place, because, heck, North Korea, and Communist China and Russia were created on this false belief of fairness.

You see, the gospel says to look objectively, the wealthy became wealthy, not be mere happenstance or luck.

If you doubt this, look at how often professional athletes and celebrities strike it rich, only to end up bankrupt.

Mike Tyson blew through $100,000,000.00 million dollars, faster than he knocked out his early opponents!

Break free the shackles this false belief binds you in!

For the gospel shows us this unfairness is the only fairness, we will ever see.

This is one of the earliest lessons, that seemingly every parent, enjoys teaching their kids, that life isn't fair!

The belief that if only Mark Cuban, and the evil rich Mr. Burns would pay his "fair share" then your life would fixed, is about as well thought out as my 3 year old nephew, putting cookies and milk out and staying up late on Christmas Eve, in hopes of catching Santa Claus!

... Sure, Homer!

The false belief in fairness is an illusion, just like David Copperfield going over Niagara Falls in a wooden barrel.

One of the first unintended consequences of higher taxes on the wealthy, will be higher prices for everyone, including the poor.

This is similar to the belief, that government health care, won't put people out of jobs that currently are employed by the health insurance companies in our Great Recession.

The plain truth is entitling anyone to anything but opportunity, is detrimental to the receiver!

After all, how fair is it, that the wealthiest section of America's population, the baby boomer generation, is also the wealthiest, yet they are entitled to free health care, social security benefits, and a whole lot more!

For the gospel tells us to choose to sacrifice, put in more effort, and make intelligent choices with our time and our life. It will develop the most valuable possession, self-reliance, an essential ingredient to all enduring success.

When you entitle someone to anything more than opportunity, you're being their Mother!

Kids and monkeys feel entitled, not grown up, mature, intelligent, and capable adults. And I'm certainly not suggesting, that we stop spending our tax revenues helping out little old Ms. Jackson, or folks that can't help themselves.

But, lets be real clear, the pain truth of our help is we give primarily for our peace of mind, not for the recipients benefit.

The belief that we are helping the poor and destitute, and feeding hungry children, in some cases is true, but often we're giving for our own selfish interest, our own peace of mind, and for the sake of our conscience.

Chapter 8.

Human Nature

It's human nature to choose the path of least resistance. It is always easier to blame circumstances and Mr. Burns for your problems.

It is infinitely more rewarding and difficult to take a hard look in the mirror, in search of ways to change and better yourself.

If you choose to search for ways, and help other people by bringing value to the market, you will be rewarded. Most often in monetary value, but this work will also give your life purpose and meaning.

Let me repeat, one of the tenets of the gospel to the good life, is to HELP and SERVE other people!

Independence

Your actions, choices, and pursuits in life are independent of anyone else choices.

If you commit yourself to successful living and financial health, and skip going to the bar with Homer on Friday, it doesn't mean Homer, Moe, or Nelson, will stop going to the bar, every Friday.

What's more likely to happen is, Homer, Moe, and Nelson, will buy your products, and services, and then complain about you being an evil rich person, and demanding you pay your "fair share" in taxes.

All the while, they will continue to merrily, spend their paycheck every week, at the so called 'Happy Hour.'

Like it or not, we are all 100%, in control of our life. We choose exactly how we respond to the circumstances that come to us, even when we're kids.

In Dennis Waitley's book, The Psychology of Winning, he tells the story of trying to feed his infant daughter strained green beans.

That plan resulted in green beans on his necktie, a trip to the dry cleaners, and uproarious laughter from his little monkey girl.

We are fortunate to have the freedom to choose how we use our time, bringing value to the marketplace, helping other people, and ultimately helping ourself.

Or waste our time and energy blaming the evil Mr. Burns, demanding someone else pay for our health care, the latest crisis in Goozulstan, and praying we strike it rich with our credit card investment in lottery tickets.

It is most productive to accept the fact that someone must pay taxes, and that paying for Homer's health insurance, sure beats the alternative of going through life in poverty, frustration, and demanding someone else pay your way!

It is human nature for people to waste their energy and time trying to rewrite the universal laws that govern mankind.

The idea of a fair utopian society, where unicorns prance on rainbows, and Stevie Wonder is playing in the background, is about as likely as the recent arrest of Chapo Guzman winning the war on drugs.

Did you know during alcohol prohibition in America, the temperance movement and the government poisoned the alcohol that was used in everyday products, like mouthwash, in hopes of preventing people from drinking it?

What happened?

You guessed it, people started dying at an alarming rate! But, rather than take a step back and reevaluate their decision, the government and temperance movement, just doubled the amount of poison in the alcohol!

I'm sure you can guess, the outcome of that decision.

For if you look objectively at history, it is easy to see the cycles and patterns repeat. The Xia Dynasty, which existed before Jesus Christ, is the first recorded society to fail at prohibition on alcohol.

Break free the shackles of fairness, the belief that giving Homer, Moe, or Nelson an equal amount of money, will have zero impact on the plain truth in the best case scenario,

Homer and Moe will be broke again in short order. And again, making credit card investments in lottery tickets!

It doesn't matter what circumstances you give some people, they will find a way to dilute themselves into believing they weren't given a fair shot.

How fair is it, that Homer, Moe, and Nelson earn the same amount of money as you, if they spend their time in the bar, when you spend your time, working, reading, and creating a better future for yourself?

Life is about choices, the world will never be fair, and who says it should be?

History seems to show the idea of "fairness" being quite detrimental to society, especially for governments. If for no other reason, than someone has to decide what is and isn't fair.

This unfairness, gives us something to work for, and strive for! Besides, how fair is it that you're born in a free country and your not a little kid living in North Korea?

How about if you can see, walk, talk, even breath, right now?

Fairness is a fantasy. All of life, is a gift, it is up to you to choose to appreciate this gift, and make something of your life and the time you have!

Or bang pots and pans, crying because the world isn't fair and Mr. Burns needs to pay more taxes, and Homer has to stop using the credit card to invest in lottery tickets!

One of the biggest differences between a successful life and misery, is the willingness to do what is difficult.

To make the decision to accept the plain truth, especially if it reveals an answer you don't want to see.

Take advantage of the opportunity your given, living in a democracy, even with it's pitfalls and shortcomings.

It is this opportunity we have, regardless of our religion, race, creed, gender, ethnicity, to achieve and create the life, we really want.

This opportunity, is what makes democracy. It single handedly, built this wonderful country of America.

It is the American dream, and responsible for every one of our ancestors, and fore fathers of this land of the brave to set out and first come here way back in 1492, and everyday, since.

Countless Americans have sacrificed their life, in payment for your opportunity, no matter if you use it or not, the tab's been paid.

Were given the chance to get ahead in life, and give our children a better future and opportunity with their life!

While America, democracy, and capitalism, aren't perfect, it sure beats the alternative of having a dictator, monarchy, communism, or any other failed government through history.

The Cannibalistic Unintended Consequences of Fairness

Did you know in the 1920's Russia experienced a famine, and received aid from President Hoover and America?

This attempt to "help" caused the hierarchy of Russia's government, to funnel these crops to their own causes, benefits, and some citizens died of starvation, as a result.

It got so bad, that cannibalism was rampant. And kids were the most sought after delight.

Mothers, tried to save their children from the pain, agony, and despair of hunger, by taking their life.

While other mothers, had to make the choice of sacrificing a child, to feed the other children ...

All the while, the people in charge of everyone getting their fair share, were busy looking out for their interests, and making sure their family weren't starving.

These leaders may have even diluted themselves into thinking this was fair.

I'm not ready to leave my life in the hands, of anyone else, and their passing whims of fairness.

One of the plain truths about mankind is, we are capable of the most amazing, wonderful, kind, loving actions, and also the exact opposite.

For the gospel says you must, take full advantage of what you've got, while you've got it, and not waste your time worrying about if its fair or not?

Besides, if you ever found the answer, it's too late to change it! Let us say thank you, and take a note from the Serenity Prayer:

"God grant me the serenity to accept the things I cannot change, the courage to change the things I can, and the wisdom to know the difference."

Chapter 9.

The Eternal Spring of Wealth

You see, in history, the wealthiest societies have been at centers of trade. Now, thanks to the internet, trade is global.

This means, you can sell something to another monkey sitting in Europe this afternoon, and Australia tonight, have PayPal do the processing, and another company fulfill, and ship your order, you can just collect the check and do a rain dance in riches.

You must create and produce something to sell, or you can always sell other monkeys products, and services for them, there a variety of ways for thee.

If you can sell directly to consumers, it's one of the most prized hunting skills in the troop today.

For the plain truth is you hear it on every episode of the Shark Tank. The Sharks always ask thee about their existing sales, because this is where life begins.

Sales are the labor pains, and with no sales, you got no business. Most men, have to sell themselves to ever get married, let alone date women.

You have to sell yourself to get a job, you have to sell your kids on doing anything, including going to the bathroom by yourself

The gospels says more important is to sell ye little ones, on living the good life, in rewarding style.

You see we are always selling our ideas, our beliefs, along with goods and services. We sell to strangers, but we also sell to loved ones.

Selling in society today is the skill of hunting in earlier civilizations. Sales are the results, the dollars, and the deer.

It is the food to feed your family, and provides the hide to clothe them. This is the prize.

Let's be clear, I'm not talking about the slimy, high pressure, car salesman type selling.

For truly effective sales, is thinking big picture, putting more importance on the value of satisfaction, repeat and referral business, along with lifetime customer value, equity, and goodwill.

For it is blasphemy to only chase the short term, quick hit, single transaction value.

For have you not heard it more effective to sheer a sheep many times, but you can skin them only once?

The gospel says creating a herd of folks, that want what you have is the fastest path to abundant and overflowing riches, as vast as the tales of King Solomon treasures.

It is much wiser, to choose the path of multiple transactions, over a lifetime, with your fellow monkeys, through building friendly, and mutually beneficial relationships, and always sell, sell, sell.

Don't neglect to ask, for ye can't receive with out asking, and ask intelligently! In this spirit, let me ask ye, to visit danmoskeluniversity.com, and sign up for free, for we have a treasure trove of wealth building tools for thee.

For this is why on Shark Tank they will say a business is only a product, and not yet a company, with an array of products and services, a list of customers, and multiple opportunities to earn revenue.

It is exponentially more valuable to your bottom line, to create relationships with people, other businesses, your customers, clients, constituents, and followers.

Don't be the "slimy" salesman, or like the politicians, promising, what you can not deliver.

The best type of selling is leading your prospect, down the path and letting your prospect buy from thee, and buy many times, instead of pressuring them to buy one time, and today only.

Good selling to putting yourself in the shoes of the customer, instead of approaching your dealings as a one time hit, scooping as many chips of the table as quick as ye can..

For instead, it should be a mutually beneficial relationship. We all must be consumers, or run the risk or using poison ivy, as a substitute for toilet paper.

Build a relationship with your customers, and they are much more likely to come back to ye, over and over again, through the course of their life, and happily give you their money, for your useful products, services, advice, and information.

The media sells people to watch their shows. The news talks about our economy being like the Great Depression, so you and I will tune in.

This is because these folks need to eat, and are paid by advertisers, who want to reach viewers like you and me.

It's commerce, and economy in action. The alternative is state sponsored television like North Korea.

Take the media reports with a grain of salt, and keep this motive at the forefront of your brain.

For the plain truth is the media must sell viewership, in order to get advertisers, so they can eat!

After all, I assure you, as bad as the winter in upstate New York is this year, the crisis in

Googlestan, it's been bad before and life will go on regardless if you know George Bush, passed a warm fart, on a rainy afternoon, or was fooled in a speech!

I would encourage ye to take a healthy step back, from total immersion in our 24 hour news day, and the latest crisis, famine, and apocalyptic event.

The media painted our recession as being the worst thing since, Conan O'Brien took over the Tonight Show.

Yet, I don't recall hearing about bread lines, and during the depression there was an alleged unemployment rate of 25%, compared to an overwhelming 6.1% in January 2014. And yes, I'm aware that the unemployment rate isn't totally accurate.

But, no bread lines and even a reported unemployment rate, 5 times as bad. I believe our unfair great recession, will go down in history as a minor blip on the radar, in comparison to the great depression of the 1920's and people actually starving to death!

Chapter 10.

The War of The Worlds

For the war of the worlds, is a radio drama performed by Orsen Wells, the same man that went on to create the widely acclaimed film Citizen Kane.

This performance originally aired on October 30th, 1938. In history, this was like April Fools day, for Halloween, it is when the older children go about and cause mischief throwing eggs at each other, and wrapping one another in ye toilet paper.

But, this performance was headline news, for the next two weeks, not because it was some fantastic piece of literature, but because of the reaction it caused among thee in America.

In spite, of the repeated disclaimers during the performance that it was a dramatization. It caused the herd to panic, stampede and frantically run around like chickens with their heads chopped off.

People were jumping in their cars and driving out into the night with no destination in mind. Others pulling over along, to the side of the road, and the masses were praying with a fever pitch asking the lord Big Banger to forgive thee.

There are even reports of some people dying from fright! It was complete pandemonium!

The herd believed the broadcast was real, Aliens were taking over the world, starting with Washington D.C.

Take heed, for the gospel says before you pass judgment, look objectively. For who knows, maybe under similar conditions, we too would be among the frantic stampede.

For did you know some experts, say America was living in a heightened state of fear, unemployment was high, we were on the brink of World War 2, and the radio was a new medium of communication.

Does this sound eerily familiar?

I think so too. The experts also say this, because some listeners didn't hear it was Aliens attacking, they heard a report about the Germans launching an attack.

For the gospel says to view with a healthy dose of skepticism, any news reports with apocalyptic headlines.

For the plain truth is George Bush may only be passing gas again, but this time, it was the type that sound like a girl scout singing, among we.

After all, how different is this, from building a bomb shelter, in case of nuclear attack?

For my wise, Grandfather told my Mom when she was a girl:

"What's the point, why would you want to live in a world after a nuclear attack. You have to live in a prison, eating hospital food, all in hopes of one day living like survivor-man, defecating in the woods, and hoping to meet someone you aren't related to, so you can procreate ... I'll pass."

I'm not suggesting a fatalistic perspective, but I am suggesting that before you go prepping for the next doomsday, and end of the world with the rest of the herd.

The gospel says DO GET BUSY living and taking advantage of the opportunities you have today, before it's too late!

The End of Days ...

What if on judgement day, your standing in front of our lord Big Danger, and you have to give an account for your time here on earth.

You meekly look up at him and claim you didn't do better, because of the OVERWHELMING unemployment rate of 6.1% and because Mr. Burns would only pay $11 million dollars in taxes every year, instead of his fair share of $12 million dollars ...

The plain truth says Dan Kennedy's idea is majestic, we should be given pictures of the American citizens we are supporting with our tax payments, just like with the charities on TV and feeding hungry orphans in third world countries.

It makes me smile and feel happier about paying my substantial "fair share" of taxes, every year!

You see there is no shortage of wealth, abundance, or success. And the people who are truly successful, are making others into real men, and independent women, every day, just like Andrew Carnegie is responsible for making over 40 men, including Charles Schwab and Napolean Hill to name but a few.

For, if we could only see, how many men, Andrew Carnegie, had a significant role in shaping, if only through the written words of Napolean Hill, I'm confident it would far outnumber the $450 million dollars he earned in the first half of his life.

Which if you didn't know, he spent the second half of his life giving all that money away. This too sounds eerily familiar, talking of Bills and Gates.

For those truly wealthy, know these laws. And for this reason, they take great caution to pass along this monkey money to their offspring, for it has the power of both good and evil.

Like Orrin C. Hudson, who started in the ghetto's of Birmingham, Alabama, and raised himself to great heights, says:

"Success is like a combination lock, once you crack the code, it doesn't matter who you are, your gender, your age, your race, or ethnicity."

Come along now, for wrap thyself in this purple silk cloak, let us dance and rejoice in the garden, among the golden pools of oil, for we have ascended the depths of trials and tribulations, to hear the words of the glorious eternal flame of fortune.

Chapter 11.

Just Do Something, Do Monkey Anything

In Robert Ringer's best-selling book, Action: Nothing Happens Until Something Moves, he says it all, in just those 5 short little words.

My own little caveat is, nothing happens until you go move a whole bunch of things!

A lot of people talk about wanting more money, and spending their time thinking about getting more money, and even wishing for more money.

I don't bloody monkey care who you are, that path for acquiring wealth, is like talking, thinking, and wanting to be better at Basketball.

Not too likely to happen, without first investing some time practicing, and actually playing Basketball.

If you want more money, and your plan is to think, wish, and talk your way to a higher income and level of wealth, your planning to fail just as the heathens.

It's like the idea of waiting to get your education. It's like saying "I'm waiting to talk to Phil Jackson, and then I'll become a better Basketball player."

Come on, man!

I recently spoke with a fellow monkey, Eddie, who shared with me he wanted to be a writer, and was going back to school.

Great Eddie, a formal education will definitely help qualify you and position you in the marketplace to get a job.

It will even train you to be a worker bee for someone else.

For, are you doing anything today, to distinguish yourself, to make even that first step out into the job market a little easier?

Eddie, said yes, he had written a book, but just needed someone to show him how to publish it, and the next steps.

That's awesome, Eddie way to go, if you want I'd be happy to publish that book, for you, here's my email address, and send it over to me and I will get it up and published by next Friday.

You know what happened ... As you've predicted, crickets.

Look, if you want to do something great, you better start right now, today, with the steps that will help you ... HERE AND NOW!

Don't be a fool, sitting on your hands waiting for someone else to educate you. For this is the forsaken path and for the gospels tells us that is a blasphemous and UNEDUCATED statement, any man can mutter.

It's no revelation, you are in need, if your plan is merely waiting! It's the same principle of ... "If only someone would show me how ... "

Don't simply think, and talk about making more money, decide once and for all, your going to get it, no matter what it takes, you will figure it out.

YOUR GOING TO GET MORE FROM
YOUR LIFE!

For the gospel saith there have been
countless men and women before you, that
have done this, there are stories of people
raising themselves up from real poverty, and
inequality ...

John D Rockefeller's dad was a scoundrel,
and on the rare times he was around, he
intentionally cheated his son in financial
dealings.

Fredrick Douglass, raised himself up from
slavery, to become an author, and a leader,
and even an advisor and friend to President
Abraham Lincoln.

He's left a significant impact, in making the
world a better place, for us today, and our
children tomorrow!

There have been bald men, fat men, stupid
men, and of course beautiful women, that have
figured it out, anyone can do it, and I promise,
you can too.

If your really ready and willing to do a whole
bunch of things, right now, this moment, if you
have yet to start, the stars are aligned, go right
bloody monkey now and commence!

Do not turn away from the tree of wealth, for thy bear fruits of fortune for anyone to only reach up and pick from thee, go now for the sound of trumpets are calling, depart from the heathens, for they walk with the beasts mark upon their forehead. Make haste, and caste the demons of procrastination, laziness, and waiting for thee out.

The time has come for your reign, most assuredly you have heard the words of our heavenly father Big Banger. Go forth, with the knowledge of the tabernacle of currency.

Chapter 12.

On The Journey

For listen to my testimony, the herd is only interested in the final destination. But, the reality is, you must bridge many small gaps and achieve a whole bunch of little milestones, before you have that big breakthrough moment of thee.

Other people will still call you an overnight success, and wonder how you did it, but like Steve Jobs said "If you really look closely, most overnight success, takes a long time."

Jack Canfield, co-author of the Chicken Soup for the Soul book series, talks about how life should be approached like an experiment.

Jack doesn't simply talk a good game, he practices what he preaches. Jack Canfield and Victor Hansen, were rejected by over 140 book publishers before, finally sealing the deal.

But, that's not the end of the story.

Jack and Victor, had to then go and promote ye book. They spent months, with minimal sales, and publicity, and one of their breakthrough moments was sending copies of the book, to all the jurors on the O.J. Simpson trial.

For this brought national publicity, and helped launched their careers, along will subsequent books, speaking engagements, and millions of dollars in royalties.

The saying about being in the right place at the right time, is sometimes true. For the gospel shows us, in order to be in the right place, you have to do all the little things, right now, today, or else you'll miss your opportunity!

And if you have missed it, don't worry, but take action today, so you don't miss it again on the morrow.

For opportunity in our great country, is like a bus, there is another one coming along every 2 minutes, but you better get ye self up off your butt and on the bus route, so you can be picked up!

For the heathens and wicked go bemoaning missed opportunity, and saying they don't know where to start, it's better to start anywhere, and JUST DO SOMETHING, otherwise you run the high chance of being impaled on the fence of indecision and ye whole life may disappear before ye eyes.

For decisions, when you have the adequate information, are not like fine red wine, where they get better with time.

Instead, it will be quite likely you will get stuck, never making a move, and be saying the same darn thing, like a cd player, stuck on repeat, forever and ever!

You see people spend years and even their whole lifetime, only thinking and merely talking about earning more money. Never doing or even reaching for their goals, or more in life!

Go now and do whatever ye have to do, your life is way to important, valuable, and can help to many other people, for you not share your skills!

The choice is yours, and it's not like you have to go make some drastic action tomorrow, though I would encourage you to.

For the gospel says the bolder the better, if your going to follow through and persevere against all difficulty!

For the wise ones of our past, Martin Luther King Jr. did saith:

"Deep in my heart I do believe we shall overcome.

And with this faith we will go out and adjourn the counsels of despair and bring new light into the dark chambers of pessimism and we will be able to rise from the fatigue of despair to the buoyancy of hope. And this will be a great America! We will be the participants in making it so.

And so as I leave you this evening I say, Walk together children! Don't you get weary!"

Other Books By Dan Moskel

Video Marketing For Entrepreneurs

Email Marketing That Works ... So You Don't Have To

The Blueprint to Affiliate Marketing

How To Create a Website Easy Button

SEO Training Manual - The 10 Golden Steps To Shower In Search Engine Traffic

* Grab a free treasure trove of wealth building tools at DanMoskelUniversity.com